The Architecture of Progress

The Architecture of Progress

Alioune Sow

CONTENTS

Reader Contract: An Agreement With Intention

Reader Contract: An Agreement With Intention
This book is not designed for speed. It is designed for structure.
What follows is not motivation, inspiration, or escape. It is an invitation to discipline—of thought, of action, and of character.
Before continuing, consider this agreement:

- I will read with patience rather than urgency.
- I will reflect honestly, even when uncomfortable.
- I will apply principles before seeking new ones.
- I accept that progress may require dismantling parts of myself I once protected.

If you are seeking affirmation, this book will disappoint you. If you are seeking alignment, continue.

Acknowledgement

Acknowledgement

This work exists because of two lives moving in parallel, bound by blood, resilience, and belief.

To Alioune Sow—who, despite incarceration, refuses to let circumstance define the limits of his mind or the scope of his vision. In a place designed to confine motion, he chose expansion. In an environment shaped by restriction, he chose reflection. This book is living proof that growth is not dependent on geography, but on intention.

To Saidou Sow, Alioune's brother and an Army Veteran, whose discipline, service, and unwavering support transformed conversation into structure and thought into form. His belief that ideas deserve stewardship, not abandonment, made this work possible.

This book stands as a testament to perseverance, brotherhood, and the quiet rebellion of thinking freely—no matter the setting.

1

Introduction: The Architecture of Progress

Progress is never accidental. It is designed—sometimes consciously, often unconsciously—through the choices we make, the values we tolerate, and the structures we uphold. Like any enduring work of architecture, meaningful progress requires intention, balance, and integrity. Without these, what appears to rise may only be temporary, fragile, or hollow.

The Architecture of Progress is not a manual for profit alone, nor is it a philosophical abstraction detached from lived experience. It is a framework for building—within ourselves, within our organizations, and within our societies—systems that endure. It invites the reader to look beyond surface-level success and examine the unseen structures that determine whether growth is sustainable or destined to collapse under its own weight.

Every civilization, institution, and individual life is constructed upon principles, whether acknowledged or ignored. Just as a building depends on the quality of its foundation, progress depends on the strength of the values that support it. When these principles erode—when integrity is compromised, accountability is avoided, or purpose is replaced by expedience—collapse is not a matter of if, but when. History repeatedly confirms this truth, not only in fallen empires and failed enterprises, but in fractured communities and unfulfilled lives.

Yet progress is possible. More than that, it is renewable—when approached with awareness. True progress does not require perfection, but alignment. It emerges when intention is matched with discipline, when ambition is guided by responsibility, and when growth is pursued without sacrificing the human cost. This book challenges the idea that progress must be ruthless, extractive, or short-sighted. Instead, it presents progress as something that can be principled, regenerative, and shared.

The architecture metaphor is intentional. Architecture is both art and science. It blends vision with constraint, creativity with rules, aspiration with gravity. A well-designed structure anticipates stress, adapts to its environment, and remains functional long after its creator is gone. In the same way, progress—when thoughtfully designed—can withstand uncertainty, evolve with time, and serve more than just its original builders.

This book is organized around three core principles, each functioning as a structural pillar. Individually, each principle offers guidance. Together, they create a framework capable of supporting growth not only in business or productivity, but in character, leadership, community,
and civilization itself. These principles are not theoretical ideals; they are practical standards, tested through experience and observation, applicable across disciplines and cultures.

The Architecture of Progress does not ask the reader to adopt a belief system, nor does it promise immediate transformation. Instead, it offers a lens—a way of seeing how progress is built, how it fails, and how it can be restored when foundations have cracked. Whether you are building a company, a family, a movement, or a life, the same question applies: What are you building on, and will it last?

The pages that follow are an invitation to examine that question honestly—and to begin designing progress with intention rather than chance.

2

The First Principle: The Philosophy of Business

Business, at its highest form, is philosophy in motion. Every enterprise—whether a global corporation or a single-person endeavor—embodies a worldview. It expresses beliefs about value, responsibility, power, and human worth through action rather than theory. Where philosophers seek truth through inquiry and dialogue, business leaders do so through decisions, trade-offs, and consequences that ripple outward into economies, communities, and futures.

The difference between philosophy and business is not intention, but discipline. Philosophy traditionally demands coherence: ideas must align, contradictions must be resolved, and assumptions must be examined. Business, by contrast, often operates under pressure—time, competition, scarcity—and in that pressure, coherence is frequently sacrificed. The result is not neutral. When discipline erodes, systems drift away from virtue and toward convenience.

Where philosophy seeks virtue as its end, business often negotiates it. Ethics become adjustable. Standards become conditional. Integrity becomes something to be referenced rather than enforced. This tension has given rise to economic systems that reward appearance over substance and profit over service—what many describe as cannibalistic capitalism.

Such systems consume trust, talent, and stability to fuel short-term gains. They may expand rapidly, but they rarely endure.

Enduring enterprises operate by a different logic. They understand that profit is not the source of sustainability, but a signal of alignment. Service precedes scale. Solutions precede monetization. Structure precedes speed. These organizations treat integrity not as a moral accessory, but as a functional requirement. Their ethics fuel innovation by creating trust. Their consistency creates resilience by reducing volatility. When integrity collapses, innovation soon follows—not because creativity disappears, but because trust does.

At the heart of sound business lies polarity—the recognition that every effect has a cause, and every cause produces consequence. Decisions shape environments, and environments shape the range of decisions that remain available. This mutual influence is inescapable. It demands responsibility, because no action exists in isolation. Every shortcut alters culture. Every compromise rewrites expectations. Every unchecked success trains future behavior.

The Five Foundational Virtues

All ecosystems—natural or human—evolve through shared virtues. These virtues are not aspirational ideals reserved for ethical discussions; they are functional necessities. Without them, systems destabilize. With them, systems self-correct.

Verity (Truth) Truth is honest feedback. It reveals what is working, what is failing, and what is being avoided. Without truth, organizations operate on illusion—rewarding narratives rather than results. Verity demands transparency, self-awareness, and the courage to confront reality as it is, not as it is marketed. Truth is often uncomfortable, but it is always corrective.

Courage Courage bridges knowing and doing. Many systems fail not because leaders lack information, but because they lack the resolve to act on it. Courage allows individuals and institutions to challenge destructive norms, accept uncertainty, and choose long-term stability over short-term comfort. Without courage, truth becomes inert.

Temperance Unchecked growth destroys ecosystems. In nature, overconsumption leads to collapse. In business, it leads to burnout, exploitation, and systemic fragility. Temperance teaches restraint, balance, and respect for limits. It ensures that progress remains regenerative rather than self-consuming. Growth that cannot pause cannot last.

Wisdom Wisdom integrates experience, foresight, and pattern recognition. It understands that no action exists in isolation and that consequences ripple across time and generations. Wisdom asks not only Can we? but Should we? and At what cost? It provides direction when data alone is insufficient.

Justice Justice sustains cohesion. In society, it ensures dignity, trust, and fairness. In business, it governs how value and burden are distributed. Without justice, cooperation erodes and conflict replaces collaboration. Systems may function temporarily through force or incentive, but they cannot endure without perceived fairness.

Together, these virtues form a self-reinforcing system. Truth reveals reality. Courage enables action. Temperance preserves balance. Wisdom guides direction. Justice sustains harmony. Remove one, and the structure weakens. Remove several, and collapse becomes inevitable.

Failure Case: Profit Without Integrity

Consider an enterprise that expands rapidly, celebrated for innovation, efficiency, and market dominance. Externally, it appears unstoppable. Internally, shortcuts replace standards. Metrics replace meaning. Communities are extracted rather than strengthened. Employees become resources to be consumed rather than people to be developed.

Over time, trust erodes. Regulation tightens. Talent departs. Public perception shifts. Growth slows, then stalls. The collapse appears sudden to outsiders, but it was neither sudden nor accidental. It was architectural—a failure of foundation rather than strategy.

Reflection: The Measure of Business

Consider an enterprise that appears successful—profitable, admired, expanding—yet leaves erosion wherever it operates. Ask yourself:

- If profit were removed, what value would remain?
- Does this system grow people, or merely consume them?
- Would it survive if integrity became non-negotiable?

Business, like philosophy, is not revealed by intention, branding, or stated values. It is revealed by consequence.

Application: Structural Alignment

Internal: Where am I tolerating misalignment because it is profitable or convenient? External: What process, partnership, or habit requires restructuring? Legacy Lens: If this model scaled for twenty years, who would it shape me—and others—into?

Progress does not fail because people aim too high. It fails because foundations are ignored

3

The Second Principle: The Art of Renovation

Renovation is not destruction—it is restoration guided by awareness. It is the decision to preserve what still serves, to repair what has weakened, and to remove what no longer supports the structure. In human growth, as in architecture, renovation begins not with force, but with honesty.

Human development mirrors the process of rebuilding. Over time, old frameworks crack. Habits that once provided stability begin to fail. Beliefs that once offered clarity prove inadequate under new weight. These fractures are not evidence of weakness; they are evidence of use. Renovation begins the moment we acknowledge what is broken without surrendering to it.

Too often, growth is framed as reinvention—burn it down, start over, become someone else. But this approach misunderstands continuity. Identity is not discarded; it is refined. Renovation honors history while refusing to be trapped by it. It asks not Who must I erase? but What must be strengthened?

Like recovery, transformation happens one day at a time. Progress under constraint—whether addiction, fear, trauma, or incarceration—demands patience and structure. In such environments, control is limited, but intention remains available. Plans made under restriction resemble flight simulation: preparation without authority over turbulence. The value lies not in perfect execution, but in disciplined rehearsal of right action.

A purpose-centered ecosystem treats others as reflections of self. This mindset may appear naïve in a competitive world conditioned by scarcity and extraction, yet it remains the only model capable of sustaining trust, cooperation, and long-term stability. Systems built on mutual recognition outlast systems built on domination. What we repeatedly do to others, we eventually normalize within ourselves.

Failure, though painful, is foundational. It reveals structural truth. Like repaired pottery mended with gold, restored systems often emerge stronger, more intentional, and more honest than they were before breaking. Healing is not denial. It is disciplined engagement with imperfection. It is the willingness to remain present with discomfort long enough for repair to occur.

Renovation follows a simple truth:

A — Accept, Adapt, Adjust Acceptance acknowledges reality without judgment. Adaptation responds creatively to constraint. Adjustment refines direction without abandoning purpose.

B — Believe and Balance Belief sustains momentum when evidence is incomplete. Balance prevents belief from becoming delusion.

C — Commitment through Discipline Discipline transforms intention into structure. Without it, insight decays into inspiration without result.

Progress is not speed—it is alignment. Rapid movement without alignment accelerates collapse. Slow movement with alignment produces durability.

Failure Case: Avoidance and Decay

When damage is ignored, systems compensate temporarily. Workarounds replace repairs. Rationalizations replace responsibility. Cracks widen quietly beneath the surface while appearances are maintained.

Eventually, collapse appears sudden—but it is never accidental. It is earned through avoidance. What was once repairable becomes irrecoverable not through impact, but through neglect.

Reflection: Restoration Over Replacement

A cracked foundation is not always a failure—it is a signal. When something breaks within you or around you, pause and ask:

- What is this failure attempting to teach?
- What must be repaired, and what must be released?
- If this were rebuilt with intention, what would it become?

Renovation begins the moment honesty replaces avoidance.

Application: Renovation in Practice

Internal: What belief or habit no longer supports who I am becoming? External: What environment must change to support restoration? Long-Term: What discipline will sustain progress when motivation fades? Renovation is not a single decision. It is a practice.

4

The Third Principle: Engineering Progress

Technological advancement without humanitarian growth is an imbalance. Innovation may accelerate, but progress loses meaning when empathy fails to keep pace with intelligence. A society can build faster machines, smarter algorithms, and more efficient systems while simultaneously neglecting the human spirit they are meant to serve. When this happens, progress becomes uneven—one community ascends while another remains trapped in survival.

History demonstrates that advancement without ethical grounding does not liberate; it concentrates. Artificial intelligence, automation, and engineering feats multiply capability, but they do not define purpose. Technology answers *how* with increasing precision, yet it remains silent on *why*. Without conscience, efficiency becomes extraction. Without compassion, optimization becomes exclusion.

Engineering progress requires more than intelligence—it requires *ethical application*. Tools are not neutral; they magnify intent. Like neural networks, humans are shaped by the data they consume: narratives, incentives, environments, and feedback loops. Unlike machines, however, humans possess agency. We choose our inputs. We decide which values to reinforce, which voices to elevate, and which outcomes we are willing to accept. In this choice lies our greatest advantage—and our greatest responsibility.

Systemic barriers often resemble flawed optimization models. They reward the wrong metrics, punish adaptability, and entrench inefficiency under the guise of order. These systems do not fail because they are complex, but because they are misaligned. Adjustment—of belief, habit, and response—allows recalibration. Growth emerges not from perfection, but from learning. When systems are willing to revise their assumptions, progress becomes possible without violence or collapse.

True progress harmonizes innovation with virtue. It recognizes that technology does not create values—it amplifies the ones already present. Power, when multiplied by machines, accelerates whatever it is attached to. With integrity, it accelerates healing, access, and understanding. Without it, power hastens collapse by scaling injustice faster than it can be repaired.

Failure Case: Intelligence Without Wisdom

Consider a system designed to optimize efficiency while ignoring dignity. Productivity rises. Outputs increase. Costs decline. On paper, success is undeniable. Yet beneath the metrics, trust erodes. People become interchangeable. Resistance grows. Innovation slows as fear replaces curiosity.

Power in such systems becomes brittle. It relies on compliance rather than consent, control rather than collaboration. Eventually, the very efficiency it prized becomes its weakness—unable to adapt because it no longer understands the humans it depends upon. The structure continues, but its spirit decays. The system's intelligence remains intact, but its wisdom is lost.

Reflection: Power With Purpose

Imagine a world where intelligence accelerates faster than wisdom. Now imagine the reverse. Ask yourself:

- Does this innovation serve dignity or dominance?
- Who benefits if this system succeeds—and who bears the cost?
- If scaled across generations, does it heal or divide?

Progress without conscience is motion without direction. Technology without humanity is speed without meaning.

To engineer progress is to design for stewardship, not control. It is to embed empathy into code, equity into access, and sustainability into aspiration. It calls for inventors who are philosophers, engineers who are humanists, and leaders who measure success not only by scale, but by stewardship of consequence.

The next frontier is not artificial—it is ethical. The most advanced systems we can build are not merely intelligent—they are aligned with human flourishing. The question is no longer whether we can build more powerful systems—but whether we can become *worthy* of them.

And worthiness cannot be automated. It must be engineered through conscience, cultivated through humility, and sustained through continual reflection. The Architect of the Future is not one who masters technology, but one who ensures it serves what is timeless.

5

The Architecture Audit

Every structure—whether built of stone or spirit—requires review. The walls we raise in conviction, the beams we align with principle, and the foundations we trust to bear our weight all demand honest inspection. To live without audit is to let erosion decide our fate.

Rate each dimension not by ambition, but by truth.

Integrity of Foundations (Truth, Justice):
What lies beneath your construction? Foundations falter when built upon convenient myths or selective honesty. Strength begins with truth—not comfort, not consensus, but what endures under pressure. Justice is not a fixture that simply stands; it is a force that continually redistributes weight toward balance. When your foundation fractures, repair does not mean concealment—it means transparency, recalibration, and the courage to rebuild without deceit.

Structural Balance (Temperance, Wisdom):
Every architecture requires symmetry—not of perfection, but of grace under tension. Temperance prevents collapse from overextension; wisdom ensures each addition serves rather than encumbers. Balance is not stillness. It is dynamic poise amidst motion. Evaluate whether your struc-

ture bends without breaking, whether your convictions can carry contradiction without crumbling. To adjust proportion is not to betray principle—it is to preserve function.

Directional Clarity (Purpose over Momentum):
A building may rise quickly yet lose its aim; momentum alone proves nothing of direction. Purpose is the compass that determines whether growth has meaning. Assess whether progress is guided or merely reactive, whether expansion serves design or distracts from it. Directional clarity transforms restlessness into trajectory—it reminds us that higher is meaningless without *why*.

Then, identify what the audit reveals:

What must be reinforced.
These are the load-bearing virtues—the unspoken commitments that hold your structure together when storms approach. Reinforcement is not addition; it is deepening where strength already roots.

What must be dismantled.
Every architecture hides weak scaffolding: habits, beliefs, or assurances that served a past blueprint but now limit expansion. To dismantle is an act of reverence—not destruction, but renewal. What no longer sustains must yield to create space for what can.

What must remain unfinished—for now.
Some rooms require patience before inhabiting. Not every angle can be perfected at once; not every height should yet be reached. The ethic of craftsmanship values timing as much as talent. Leaving something unfinished is an acknowledgment that evolution is not shame—it is design.

Revisit this audit annually—not to seek flaw, but to honor growth. The architecture of self, like any enduring structure, survives by maintenance, not memory. Each year, return with clearer eyes and steadier hands. Tighten what has loosened. Soften what has hardened. Align, amend, sustain.

Your structure is never final—it is faithful.

6

Closing Reflections: Legacy, Virtue, and Evolution

Virtue is not rewarded by society—it is sustained by integrity. The world's recognition is fleeting, but the conscience remains steadfast, measuring worth not by applause, but by effort aligned with principle. True virtue asks not to be seen; it asks to be *lived*. It is the quiet discipline of choosing right action when convenience would suffice, of building inward strength even when no audience remains to witness it.

Transformation is often invisible. Rehabilitation requires preparation, education, and resilience. Renewal cannot be rushed—it evolves through repetition, confrontation, and grace. The cracks we conceal often become the channels through which wisdom flows. In reclaiming the self, each setback becomes an architect of depth; each lesson, a quiet revolution within. Growth is not always spectacular—it often hides beneath the surface, shaping endurance through the slow architecture of patience.

Yet the pursuit of virtue remains a personal endeavor, defined not by recognition, but by consistency. The rhythm of goodness is not marked by applause, but by return—returning to honesty after error, to compassion after anger, to faith after doubt. Consistency is the proof of transformation, not its ornament. In a society driven by display, consistency remains a quiet rebellion—a vow to sustain what is right even as the world drifts toward spectacle.

Just as illumination is meaningless without application, confinement without evolution is stagnation. Insight, if not embodied, becomes complacency. Knowledge demands movement; wisdom demands translation into action. To learn without changing is to decorate the mind without expanding the spirit. Transformation fulfills itself only when reflection becomes participation—when thought becomes structure, when intention is tested by the weight of practice.

Progress—personal or collective—demands participation. To watch idly is to consent to decay. To act—even imperfectly—is to contribute to the unfinished work of human dignity. The Architecture of Progress is not a destination. It is a discipline. A commitment to build wisely, restore intentionally, and evolve with purpose. Every generation inherits both the ruins and the blueprints of those before them; every individual becomes a craftsman of continuity.

Legacy is not what we accumulate—it is what we strengthen for those who come next. Wealth fades, names erode, monuments collapse—but the virtues we pass on remain the invisible scaffolding of civilization. Legacy is measured by the courage we inspire, the wisdom we preserve, and the compassion we transmit through our presence. It is less an inheritance than an invitation—to continue the work, to refine what is possible, to ensure that progress does not lose its moral direction.

And in that strengthening, we discover continuity: that our actions, humble or grand, become patterns within a greater design. The integrity we protect today becomes the foundation of tomorrow's restoration. Virtue outlives applause. Progress outpaces possession. Legacy endures not through monuments, but through minds awakened to build anew.

To evolve is to remember that every structure—ethical, emotional, societal—must be maintained. The architecture of progress demands both strength and surrender: strength to hold its weight, and surrender to rebuild when the design no longer serves. It is an act of stewardship, not conquest.

The end of one era is always the foundation of the next. And so, evolution becomes an act of faith—the belief that what we create with integrity will invite others to continue the work with hope. In that quiet handoff, the human story endures.

Progress is not accidental. It is designed.

The Architecture of Progress is a disciplined framework for building a life, organization, and society that can endure pressure without collapse. Rejecting surface-level motivation and empty affirmation, this book invites readers into a deeper examination of how progress is actually constructed—and why it so often fails.

Through three core principles—**The Philosophy of Business, The Art of Renovation, and Engineering Progress**—the book explores how values become systems, how failure reveals structural truth, and how innovation loses meaning when it outpaces ethics. Drawing from philosophy, leadership, technology, and lived experience, it reframes growth as an architectural process: one that demands integrity in its foundations, balance in its expansion, and purpose in its direction.

At its core are five foundational virtues—**Truth, Courage, Temperance, Wisdom, and Justice**—presented not as moral ideals, but as functional requirements for sustainable progress. When these virtues are ignored, systems decay. When they are honored, progress becomes regenerative rather than extractive.

This is not a book to be consumed quickly. It is a book to be applied deliberately.

For readers willing to confront misalignment, dismantle what no longer serves, and design their progress with intention, The Architecture of Progress offers not answers—but a structure strong enough to hold them.

What are you building on—and will it last?

www.ingramcontent.com/pod-product-compliance
Lightning Source LLC
LaVergne TN
LVHW101618210926
848480LV00009B/826

9798295644863